GARDEN GUIDES

HERBS & THE KITCHEN GARDEN

GARDEN GUIDES

HERBS & THE KITCHEN GARDEN

KIM HURST

Illustrations by
BRENDA STEPHENSON

This edition first published in 1996 by
Parragon
13 Whiteladies Road
Clifton
Bristol, BS8 1PB

Reprinted 1999

Produced by
Robert Ditchfield Ltd
Combe Court
Kerry's Gate
Hereford HR2 0AH

ISBN 0 75252 446 1

A copy of the British Library Cataloguing in Publication Data is
available from the Library.

Typeset by Action Typesetting Ltd, Gloucester
Colour origination by Mandarin Offset Ltd, Hong Kong
Printed and bound in Italy

ACKNOWLEDGEMENTS

Most of the photographs were taken in the author's nursery and garden, The Cottage Herbery, Mill House,
Boraston Ford, near Tenbury Wells. The publishers would also like to thank the many people and organizations
who have allowed photographs to be taken for this book, including the following:

Mr and Mrs Terence Aggett; Barnsley House; Batemans (National Trust); Lallie Cox, Marlcliff, Woodpeckers,
Bidford-on-Avon; Mrs L. Davies; Mr and Mrs K. Dawson, Chennels Gate, Eardisley; Richard Edwards, Well
Cottage, Blakemere; Lance Hattatt, Arrow Cottage, Weobley; Mr and Mrs James Hepworth, Elton Hall; Hergest
Croft Gardens; The Hop Pocket, Bishops Frome; Mr and Mrs B. Howe; Merdon Manor; Mottisfont Rose Gardens
(National Trust); Mr and Mrs R. Norman, Marley Bank, Whitbourne; Mrs R. Paice, Bourton House; Mary-Ann
Robinson; Royal Botanic Gardens, Kew; RHS Garden, Wisley; Torwood, Whitchurch; Mrs Trevor-Jones, Preen
Manor; David Wheeler, The Neuadd; Mrs Geoffrey Williams, Close Farm, Crockham Hill; Mrs David Williams-
Thomas, The Manor House, Birlingham; Woodlands, Bridstow; York Gate, Leeds.

CONTENTS

Poisonous Plants

In recent years, concern has been voiced about poisonous plants or plants which can cause allergic reactions if touched. The fact is that many plants are poisonous, some in a particular part, others in all their parts. For the sake of safety, it is always, without exception, essential to assume that no part of a plant should be eaten unless it is known, without any doubt whatsoever, that the plant or its part is edible and that it cannot provoke an allergic reaction in the individual person who samples it. It must also be remembered that some plants can cause severe dermatitis, blistering or an allergic reaction if touched, in some individuals and not in others. It is the responsibility of the individual to take all the above into account.

We would also like to point out that although many herbs have a medicinal reputation, it is advisable to check with your doctor before treating yourself.

How to Use This Book

Where appropriate, approximate measurements of a plant's height have been given, and also the spread where this is significant, in both metric and imperial measures. The height is the first measurement, as for example 1.2m × 60cm/4 × 2ft. However, both height and spread vary so greatly from garden to garden since they depend on soil, climate and position, that these measurements are offered as guides only. This is especially true of trees and shrubs where ultimate growth can be unpredictable.

The following symbols are also used throughout the book:
  ○ = thrives best or only in full sun
  ◑ = thrives best or only in part-shade
  ● = succeeds in full shade
  E = evergreen
Where no sun symbol and no reference to sun or shade is made in the text, it can be assumed that the plant tolerates sun or light shade.

Plant Names

For ease of reference this book gives the common name by which a herb or vegetable is generally known. Botanical names are also given where these may be of help.

Herbs and the Kitchen Garden

Sweet bay with the berries of *Iris foetidissima* make a charming winter wall hanging.

(*Opposite*) This exuberant formal garden has roses mingling with the scents of herbs.

Even the smallest garden can include herbs. Many are ornamental, most are fragrant and almost all accommodating enough to be tucked into odd corners. In addition, the culinary herbs can turn even the simplest everyday meal into a treat. Add to this a few of your own home-grown vegetables, freshly picked from the garden, and you have the makings of a feast – which will also be a healthy one.

Quite apart from this, growing and eating food of your own is economical, gives much pleasure and a sense of satisfaction. It need not be ambitious. Indeed, it is better to be cautious and selective at first, growing only crops you think will thrive in your situation (a precaution that is worth taking to avoid mistakes and disappointments). Instead, it might be something as simple and easy as a bunch of radishes, but pulling that first fresh bunch on a sunny day, brushing away the soil, washing the handful of bright red roots and munching them with a salad can give pleasure that is out of proportion to the effort.

GROWING HEALTHY FOOD

Growing your own produce also means that you have a say in what goes into it. You can make the choice to raise your crops organically, using only good natural methods, knowing that what you are eating has been grown without a chemical in sight. This is purely an individual decision that everyone makes for him or herself but it must be said that raising

A herb garden in late summer.

your own herbs and vegetables is an excellent opportunity to produce healthy and nutritious food which is free of chemicals. All that is needed is a good humus-rich soil, water, sunshine and your time. If your earth is difficult, raised beds are a very good substitute as you can fill them with another type of soil or a good organic compost. If reclaiming an old overgrown garden, start with a small area which can be easily managed. Once it is under control, move on to the next patch, and in this way you won't get discouraged.

Many of the herbs and flowers mentioned in the book attract beneficial insects into the garden, which in turn helps control pests. If you create an area within your garden for these plants, or include them amongst your vegetables, then the garden will in time develop its own natural balance.

A SMALL PLOT

This book has been written with the small garden in mind, for grand gardens do not have a monopoly on herbs and kitchen produce. With careful preparation and planning, even the tiniest garden can yield a good range of fresh food.

Town dwellers, who feel perhaps that they are limited in what food they can grow, need not despair. With a little thought and determination, successful crops can be raised in pots, tubs, barrels, old sinks and window boxes. Examples of these are shown in the chapter on containers, and they can range from edible flowers and salad crops to potatoes, root crops and brassicas. Parsley, nasturtiums and mixed-leaf lettuce will all happily grow in window boxes and large wall pots.

Variety of leaf is a very great asset in herb gardens, especially when accompanied by the bright flowers of this nasturtium.

A small and beautifully designed herb garden showing how important is attention to details like paving and seating.

THE DECORATIVE GARDEN

Pattern, form and shape can be created with different colours and foliage of herbs and vegetables alike. The brilliant red stalks of the rhubarb chard, marbled squashes, yellow zucchini, and frilly endive will provide a colourful patchwork of edible delights. Include vegetables and herbs that grow tall or ones that can be trained to climb (such as hops, marrows and beans) for these will add a vertical dimension to the garden, but remember to leave room around their roots where you can sow quick-growing crops of rocket, landcress and radishes.

The appearance of the pretty and ever popular potager can be easily achieved in the small garden without the use of dwarf box to hedge its ornamental beds. Instead you can plant hedge germander (*Teucrium chamaedrys*) to create neat kerbs; alternatively, wooden boards, slates and bricks can be used to contain the soil. Here imaginative design and planting are the secret to the overall look.

PLEASURE OF THE HARVEST

Harvesting your crops of herbs, flowers and vegetables starts early in the spring reaching an ultimate crescendo in the autumn.

In the spring you can gather fresh chives, chervil and parsley for soups, omelettes and salads; sweet cicely leaves for removing the tartness from rhubarb; hop shoots to steam

(*Left*) Curving paths and small box hedges contain beds of herbs alternating with colourful ornamentals.

(*Right*) Another view of the same garden. The standard rose 'The Fairy' provides a tall focal point amongst the lower compartments of herbs and vegetables.

and add to salads and savoury flans (or pick them to be eaten on their own with butter, when they are called poor man's asparagus, though I personally regard them as food for the gods!). This is also the season to pick the fresh new leaves of good king henry which is rich in minerals and iron. Steamed with fresh nettle tops and added to a cheese flan, it is a spring tonic for all.

Quickly summer moves in with an abundance of salad crops, decorative red lettuce, wild blue chicory, and blue borage self-seeded amongst the carrots and beetroot. Bees hum round the flat heads of the elegant dill, moving down to drink from the bright orange faces of the pot marigolds. All add to that

heady summer feeling. One of my hardest jobs at this time of the year is to remove the perfect blooms of my roses, cornflowers and the like, but if I am to savour their delights in the winter they need to be collected at their best and dried quickly to preserve their beauty and scent for pot-pourri.

Lavender, southernwood, balm and sage are a few of the other herbs which are collected in summer for their aromatic properties. They should be hung in bunches and dried to be used throughout the winter.

In early autumn the harvest really gathers speed. Now it is a rush to complete all the tasks that need to be done: picking beans and peas, gathering onions and garlic, all the

freezing, drying, bottling and making of chutneys, pickles and other preserves. This always turns into a race against time before the onset of the first frosts. Yet it is worth it to capture all your work and enjoy the flavours in the winter as you have through the other seasons.

As I collect my herbs and flowers through the seasons, in my mind I piece together some of the decorations I shall make for autumn and winter with the dried material. These include sachets, pillows, wreaths, wall-hangings and many more delights as shown in the chapter on decoration.

We have now come full circle to the time when, after a good wholesome meal made with the fruits of your labour and maybe some home-made strawberry wine, you can sit down with some seed catalogues by the fire. At this point it is tempting to excite the imagination with wonderful names of plants from exotic places, and to dream up elaborate schemes and dishes with all the herbs, vegetables and fruits. But be warned that these do not always work and, for my part, past disappointments have taught me better. I would suggest that you choose wisely, grow for your needs and pick varieties that are not so readily available in the shops. This is now my motto and it works. Knowing this, you can plan next year's crops with the insight that nothing can be more satisfying than growing your own.

1. Herb and Kitchen Gardens

The herb and kitchen garden can be visually satisfying but it also appeals to the senses of taste and smell.

TRADITIONAL KITCHEN GARDENS

TRADITIONAL KITCHEN GARDENS were born out of necessity more than for their aesthetic appeal, with every inch of land allotted to the production and rotation of crops to feed the family for a year. Even after a long day's work there would be no rest until the daily jobs in the garden had been done.

Growing your kitchen garden in the traditional style of rows eases a somewhat labour-intensive system when it comes to sowing, hoeing, growing and harvesting. This layout also makes crop rotation easier to follow.

This modern kitchen garden has been subdivided to make access easy. This system will also make rotation easier.

◆ *The strong lines of this garden mean that it looks handsome even with areas of bare earth.*

TRADITIONAL KITCHEN GARDENS

Terracotta pots like this will give you an early crop of rhubarb by 'forcing' the stems to seek the light. Much of the charm of a kitchen garden lies in the use or adaptation of traditional methods like this one.

The same garden two months later. Cropping has begun and flowers for cutting are in full bloom.

◆ *Note the long flowering season of the chives in the foreground.*

POTAGERS

A POTAGER, although often associated with the gardens of large country houses, is easily adapted to the small garden. Careful planning, planting and keeping the basis of the design simple is the key. Vegetables, herbs and flowers are planted as a design to give colour and form.

Good pathways are essential for easy tending and harvesting. A wheelbarrow's breadth is ideal. Gravel, brick or bark are good mediums.

◆ *The paths of a potager both organize it and create a pleasing design.*

Standard gooseberry bushes are often planted as a centrepiece in a small potager bed to give it a central focus. Although the appearance of the bush is crucial in these ornamental kitchen gardens, it can be very productive and allows for easy harvesting of the fruits.

Beds in a potager can be edged by the path or by a small hedge – here, box surrounds this lavender bed.

◆ *Chives, feverfew or decorative cabbages would make a softer planted edge.*

A potager can combine the satisfaction of straight lines of productive crops with artistic arrangement of paths and plants.

◆ *The edges of this bed are lined with clipped young box plants.*

POTAGERS

Standard roses can be useful design features in a potager, giving height, colour and scent.

Another way of lifting the eye is to install arches on which climbing beans or courgettes (zucchini) can be grown.

Ornamental cabbages in pinks, whites and greens are a popular way of decorating a potager bed, either as edging or to create their own pattern.

Lettuces can also be grown in many forms from deep ruby reds to pale greens.

If you are planning a productive potager, think in terms of vegetables and herbs you most enjoy when they are absolutely fresh. Easily grown vegetables include beetroot, carrots, courgettes (zucchini), dwarf French beans, lettuce, radishes and spinach.

CREATING A HERB GARDEN

1. You can make a herb garden in a very small area and still grow a useful number of plants. Most herbs prefer an open sunny position, but will tolerate some shade. Ensure the ground is well prepared and all weeds removed.

2. Subdivide the area to make access easy. The garden will also be more appealing if you can partition it off or give it some shape through either hard materials or patterned planting. Here a simple brick path has been laid to a hard area in the corner and tiles mark the near edge.

3. Place the herbs in position with taller plants towards the back. If the soil is heavy, incorporate some organic material and grit when planting as well as a slow-release fertiliser. Water in and keep the bed weeded whilst the plants establish themselves.

4. This is the same bed three months later with many herbs already cropping and some blooming. The gaps which had been left in the path are already filled with creeping chamomile and thyme and on a sunny summer's day the whole area is a bouquet of fragrance.

HERB GARDENS DO NOT REQUIRE A HUGE AREA. Just a few plants of thyme, mint, parsley, and sage make a valuable contribution to the kitchen but take up very little space. If you are able to grow more, you can design a close-knit pattern of herbs in any shape you please.

A SMALL HERB GARDEN

The designer of this small walled garden has taken great trouble over laying the paths and placed a seat where one can enjoy the scents of the plants in such an enclosed area to the full.

This is a traditional 'wheel' herb bed with four spokes to divide it up.

◆ *The hedging here is of clipped ivy.*

Charming small herb beds surrounding two cherry trees as part of a larger garden.

◆ *Hard surfaces help 'stabilize' the floppy nature of some herbs.*

EDGES *and* HEDGES

There are two types of hedging. The clipped formal hedge can be made with box, santolina, hyssop or hedge germander. For the informal look, plant lavender, chives, winter savory and feverfew.

Traditionally herb and kitchen gardens had some sort of formal hedging and this was both a practical and decorative means of shaping the garden.

The knot gardens, popular in the sixteenth and seventeenth centuries, were the result of intricate artistry using hedging plants to create patterned gardens with little or no infill planting. Evergreen plants such as box, hyssop, lavender, santolina, savory and thyme would have been used.

Rock hyssop (*Hyssopus aristatus*) – Dwarf variety of hyssop with an interesting spiky, upright habit. A useful plant for hedging, it needs little attention and minimal clipping. Deep blue flowers midsummer.

Dwarf box hedges interweaving to form the intricate pattern of a knot garden, creating spaces for planting herbs or siting pots.

◆ *Such a knot will take about three years to establish, but needs regular clipping.*

Box (*Buxus sempervirens*)
Hardy evergreen shrub.
'Suffruticosa' is a dwarf
form. Take cuttings in
spring or autumn. E

Hyssop (*Hyssopus officinalis*)
Hardy evergreen shrub.
Blue, pink or white-
flowered forms. Trim in
spring to keep its shape. E

Cotton lavender (*Santolina chamaecyparissus*) Good
dense bush which clips well.
'Nana' is a compact variety,
good for knot gardens. E

Lavender (*Lavandula*) In
small gardens try a compact
variety like *L. angustifolia*
'Hidcote' or 'Munstead'. E

Hedge germander
(*Teucrium chamaedrys*) Bright
pink flowers midsummer.
Ideal knot garden plant. E

Winter savory (*Satureja montana*) Tough narrow
aromatic leaves, white
flowers. Prune in late
spring. E

Feverfew (*Tanacetum parthenium*) Gives a softer
edge. Easy to grow with
appealing white daisy
flowers.

Chives (*Allium schoenoprasum*) Useful
edging and companion
plant to keep away pests.
Divide every second year.

Compact marjoram
(*Origanum vulgare*
'Compactum') Decorative
purple/pink flowers and a
tidy tight habit.

EDGES *and* HEDGES

CLIPPING – an essential
regular job. As most of the
plants are aromatic, the
clippings can be gathered
up, dried and used for pot-
pourri. Before you begin to
clip, lay down a piece of
cloth for the clippings to
fall on, making it easier to
gather them up especially if
you have gravel pathways.

Southernwood
(*Artemisia abrotanum*)
Woody shrub with finely
divided, heavily scented
leaves. Hedging for a large
border or pathway. Clip
back hard in late spring to
keep its shape. Semi-E

CARPETING HERBS

Prepare the area to be planted with carpeting herbs thoroughly, removing all weeds, especially perennial kinds which would be difficult to eradicate later.

HERBS THAT CAN CREATE A CARPETING EFFECT offer the bonus of suppressing weeds as well as giving off aroma. Planted along edges of pathways they creep along naturally, softening the overall look. Enhance a paved area by planting in the cracks chamomile, Corsican mint or compact thymes. Alternatively, plan a Persian carpet of textures and colours in a gravel garden or area bounded by stone.

***Thymus serpyllum* 'Snowdrift'** The thymes are ideal spreading shrubs for covering sunny areas in gravel gardens, patios, rock gardens or anywhere you need a fragrant evergreen mat.

◆ *Propagate by taking softwood cuttings in summer.*

Corsican mint (*Mentha requienii*) For small areas, a creeper with a peppermint scent. Tiny leaves and purple flowers. Semi-E

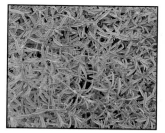

Creeping savory (*Satureja spicigera*) Ground hugging, highly aromatic. Needs a well drained, sunny position. White flowers. E

Thymus serpyllum coccineus The numerous small flowers of some forms of thyme can almost totally obscure the tiny leaves. E

CARPETING HERBS

For shady areas and under trees sweet woodruff (*Galium odoratum* syn. *Asperula*) thrives well, making a bright green carpet, covered in small white flowers in early summer.

Creeping pennyroyal (*Mentha pulegium*) Bright green foliage and mauve flowers, said to keep ants at bay. Prefers moist soil.

Lawn chamomile (*Chamaemelum nobile* 'Treneague') Bright green, apple-scented foliage, non-flowering. E

This urn is surrounded by a dense planting of chamomile at the centre of a formal herb garden.

◆ *Replanting is sometimes necessary as plants die out in a chamomile carpet.*

POTTED HERB GARDENS

HERBS ARE SUCH GOOD SUBJECTS FOR POTS. Most enjoy the restriction and well-drained medium that can be provided in a pot. With their various decorative foliages and delicate flowers, they turn a dull terrace, veranda or patio into something to appreciate and admire.

PLANTING UP A POT

Use good nutrient-rich compost, preferably organic peat-free, and add to this a handful each of grit and coarse sand for drainage. Fill half of the pot with compost, then start to plant from the centre outwards.

Suitable plants would be one well shaped rosemary, surrounded by parsley, chives, oregano, winter savory, sage and French tarragon, interspersed with three trailing nasturtiums for colour and use in salads.

Containers for herbs do not have to be art objects in themselves. Old enamel basins, even modern plastic bowls that have sprung leaks will make perfectly good little herb gardens. Ensure that there is proper drainage by drilling holes in the base.

Standard bay tree Of all the herbs, a potted standard bay tree is the most prized. Snipping leaves off for culinary use helps to keep the shape, if you use your eye correctly. Re-pot and dress every year. Feed regularly. E

One great advantage of a potted herb garden is that you don't have to cultivate areas of land. Replacing a plant is very simple.

◆ *Invasive herbs like mint, bergamot, oregano and lemon balm can be contained to prevent them smothering other plants.*

27

POTTED KITCHEN GARDENS

SMALL-SCALE KITCHEN GARDENS can be very productive in containers, such as old sinks, wooden boxes, troughs, buckets, enamel bread bins and hanging baskets. Salads, courgettes, dwarf beans, salad herbs and cascading tiny tomatoes, if fed and watered well, will give a good crop.

Old wheelbarrows are very popular containers for ornamental plants, but can just as easily be made into small kitchen gardens.

◆ *Ensure that contained plants are watered regularly and that they have an adequate supply of fertilizer.*

Tomatoes are probably more often grown in pots than in the open ground. They need warmth and sunshine for fruits to develop and ripen.

Green peppers (capsicums) are also particularly suited to pot culture. Pots can be moved to take advantage of sunny positions and the plants fed and tended more easily.

Runner beans growing up a central support in the pot. If raised in the warm in the spring, the plants will crop earlier than outdoor sowings.

A wall pot like this is all you need to grow a few simple herbs.

Even if you have just a small concrete yard, you can still grow fresh peas.

It is worth keeping a pot of mixed salad by the kitchen door to add some fresh leaves to summer meals.

◆ *Grow claytonia in a pot for a good winter salad plant.*

This vegetable bed has been 'contained' with timbers – not movable, but it does make maintenance easier.

2. THE GROWING YEAR

*Each season brings with it the tasks and
pleasures of growing, tending,
harvesting and finally resting.*

PERENNIAL HERBS

EARLY SPRING SEES THE FIRST GREEN SHOOTS of the sweet cicely pushing through, to begin another year's cycle. Other perennial herbs have had to contend with winter weather above ground – rosemary, sage, thyme, all evergreens. Chives, mint and marjoram appear gingerly until a brief warm spell spurs them into earnest growth with the rest of the perennials following.

Herbs thrive in conditions similar to their natural habitat, often of Mediterranean kind, so ideally they should have plenty of sunshine and free-draining soil.

In reality not all of us have those conditions. Raised beds are a good solution to soil problems: you can create the right medium in which to grow your herbs. Add organic nutrients to a mix of garden soil, organic compost and grit. Make sure when buying in soil that it is clear of any damaging pests and diseases.

The ground-cover rose 'Raubritter' and feathery bronze fennels make a pretty combination.

The blue-green of rue on the right adds to the subtle tones and shapes of this bed.

Lavender and the fresh green of spearmint complement the biennial evening primrose (*Oenothera biennis*).

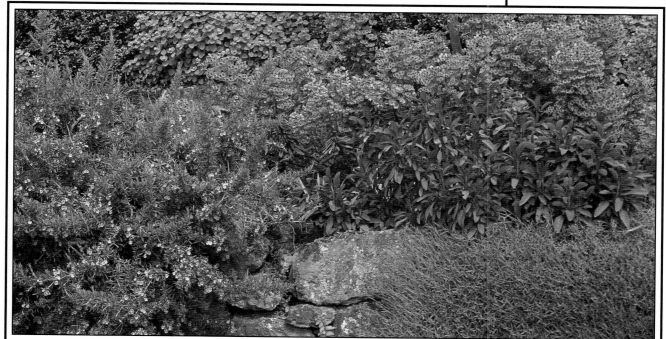

Handsome clumps of blue-flowered rosemary and purple-leaved sage add to the varied textures of this border.

◆ *A planting of perennial herbs like this requires minimal upkeep.*

PERENNIAL HERBS

The following herbs will tolerate moist shade – angelica, chives, feverfew, balm, lovage, mints, sorrel and woodruff.

Always grow culinary herbs away from pet areas and roadside pollution. After all, you will be eating them.

Clumps of chives can be dug up and divided in early spring. This helps to keep them young and their growth productive.

Always use scissors to cut chives both in gathering and preparing in the kitchen. This is much the easiest way to deal with them.

YARROW
(*Achillea millefolium*)
Ancient wound and tonic herb. Infuse flowers to make a facial steambath. Flowers dry well for winter decoration.
○, up to 1 × 1m/3 × 3ft

CHIVES
(*Allium schoenoprasum*)
Used for many hundreds of years for their delicate onion flavour and abundant production of leaves from early spring to the beginning of winter.
○, 23 × 15cm/9 × 6in

◆ *The fresh leaves have many uses in salads, soups, sandwiches, omelettes, soufflés, dips and flans.*

GARLIC CHIVES
(*Allium tuberosum*)
Well drained soil necessary. Also known as Chinese chives. Slower growing than common chives with a shorter season. Leaves long and flat with a distinctive garlic taste.
○, 30 × 20cm/1ft × 8in

ANGELICA
(*Angelica archangelica*)
Grow in deep moist soil. Majestic short-lived perennial. Young stalks can be candied or added to jams and jellies for a different taste. 1.8 × 1m/ 6 × 3ft

HORSERADISH
(*Armoracia rusticana*)
A rampant grower. Documented for thousands of years as a food flavouring. The roots are freshly grated for sauces. Use sparingly.
60cm/2ft × indefinite spread.

PERENNIAL HERBS

FRENCH TARRAGON
(*Artemisia dracunculus*)
Needs a warm sheltered place, protection in winter and good drainage. Grows well in a cold greenhouse. Good vinegar herb. ○, up to 1m × 60cm/3 × 2ft

COSTMARY
(*Balsamita major*, syn. *Tanacetum balsamita*)
Known also as alecost, once used to flavour ale. Monks used a leaf in their bibles as a bookmarker and insect repellant.
1m × 60cm/3 × 2ft

FENNEL
(*Foeniculum vulgare*)
Grow in well drained loam. Tall elegant plant. Mild liquorice flavour. Use young leaves and stalks for soups, sauces, mixed salads and with fish dishes.
2.2 × 1m/7 × 3ft

Sow only fresh seed of angelica for maximum germination.

The flowerheads of angelica make excellent winter decorations when dried.

Don't plant fennel near dill or coriander as cross-pollination can occur and seed production of the fennel will suffer.

Many of these herbs can play a useful part in mixed borders. Architectural plants like angelica, fennel and lovage are a strong presence and add height to the planting. The different blue hues of lavender, rosemary and catmint are particularly valuable when repeated at intervals along a border. The same is true of wormwood, curry plant and sage.

SWEET WOODRUFF
(*Galium odoratum* syn. *Asperula odorata*)
A creeping woodland herb used to enhance the taste of white wine. Dried it smells of new mown hay and is good for pot-pourri and herb pillows. 30cm/1ft

◆ *It makes a charming carpeting plant for under trees, as it tolerates a degree of shade.*

CURRY PLANT
(*Helichrysum angustifolium*)
Needs light soil. Attractive silver foliage plant with small yellow flowers. Distinctive curry scent. Good edging plant. Flowers dried for pot-pourri.
○, E, 60 × 60cm/2 × 2ft

PERENNIAL HERBS

Chop the leaves of lemon balm with a little dill, mix into sour cream and serve with fresh salmon.

Balm planted near hives keeps the bees happy and relaxed.

If bay was in abundance the branches and leaves used to be burnt on an open fire to refresh and cleanse the room.

A bay leaf in the flour bin keeps away the weevil.

HOP
(*Humulus lupulus*)
Hop flowers are used for ale. Pick tender young shoots in spring, steam and serve with butter, like asparagus. For humus-rich soil. 7 × 2m/23 × 6ft

HYSSOP
(*Hyssopus officinalis*)
Good hedging plant and bee plant. Monks used it to flavour wine and liqueurs. Can be dried, and used in pot-pourri.
○, E, 60cm × 1m/2 × 3ft

BAY
(*Laurus nobilis*)
Often preferred as a standard bush. Dried leaves in casseroles, game dishes, paté, marinades, soups. Crumbled leaves in pot-pourri. Not fully hardy.
○, E, 7 × 1.5m/23 × 5ft

LAVENDER
(*Lavandula* spp.)
Aromatic foliage and flowers. Dry flowers when first out. Pot-pourri, scented sachets and perfume. (See also 'Edible Flowers').
○, E, up to 1 × 1m/3 × 3ft

LOVAGE
(*Levisticum officinale*)
Distinctive yeasty celery flavour. Leaves for soups, stews, casseroles, marinades. Use seeds for bread, to sprinkle on salads, or make a savoury tea.
2.1 × 1m/7 × 3ft

LEMON BALM
(*Melissa officinalis*)
Good bee plant. Musky lemon scent to leaves which taste good in salads, soups, herb bread, cakes and sauces. 60 × 60cm/2 × 2ft

APPLEMINT
(*Mentha suaveolens*)
Woolly textured leaves with a delicate minty apple scent. Use finely chopped in salads and dressings.
◑, 1m × indefinite spread

GINGERMINT
(*Mentha × gentilis*)
Leaf-tips used to decorate food. Tear small amounts of leaves into a mixed salad, dress with olive oil.
60cm/2ft × indefinite spread

PEPPERMINT
(*Mentha × piperita*)
Mainly used as a digestive tea. Dried for herbal sachets and pillows to ease colds and blocked sinuses. Pot-pourri.
45cm/1½ft × indefinite spread

MOROCCAN MINT
(*Mentha spicata* 'Moroccan')
Sharp mint flavour makes excellent mint sauce and jelly. Shred a few leaves into green salad and dress with lemon juice. 45cm/1½ft × indefinite spread

SPEARMINT
(*Mentha spicata*)
Often known as garden mint. Mint sauce and jelly. Add to cooked vegetables and salads. Dries well. Use dried flowering tops for herbal decorations. 45cm/1½ft × indefinite spread

PENNYROYAL
(*Mentha pulegium*)
Two types, upright and creeping. Strong peppermint scent. Good for paved areas. Insect repellant.
15 × 30cm/6in × 1ft

PERENNIAL HERBS

As its name suggests, lovage was used as a love charm and aphrodisiac. Czechoslovakian girls hung a bag of lovage around their necks when out courting.

A handful of mint put into a warm bath is supposed to comfort and strengthen the nerves.

Mint was once used to keep vermin out of the house where it was strewn on the floor and stuffed into bedding.

PERENNIAL HERBS

SWEET CICELY
(*Myrrhis odorata*)
First herb to appear in the spring, last to die back in the autumn. Leaves are anise-flavoured. Cooked with tart fruits reduces acidity. 60 × 60cm/2 × 2ft

CATMINT
(*Nepeta cataria*)
True herbal catmint, not so decorative as purple-flowered *N. × faassenii*. Unusual pungent scent which encourages the attention of cats, often to its detriment.
60 × 45cm/2 × 1½ft

POT MARJORAM
(*Origanum onites*)
A good herb for seafood soups, eggs, fish, meat, poultry, game, stews, vegetarian dishes, salads and sauces.
60 × 60cm/2 × 2ft

BERGAMOT
(*Monarda didyma*)
Tea herb. Dried whole plant in pot-pourri. Fresh leaves sparingly in salads and dressings. Good bee and butterfly plant. For well-drained soil.
1m × 60cm/3 × 2ft

OREGANO
(*Origanum vulgare*)
Use leaves for Mediterranean dishes, pizza, tomatoes, *bouquet garni*, seafood casseroles and roasting meats. Dry flowering stalks for decoration.
15 × 60cm/6in × 2ft

BISTORT
(*Persicaria bistorta*)
Once used as a wound herb. Early spring use young leaves in salads or steamed as a vegetable.
1m × 60cm/3 × 2ft

COWSLIP
(*Primula veris*)
A favourite spring flower. Flowers used in jam, wine and pickled. Dried flowers and powdered roots in pot-pourri. 23 × 15cm/9 × 6in

PERENNIAL HERBS

ROSEMARY
(*Rosmarinus officinalis*)
Much loved for its cleansing properties. Many varieties including pink and white flowered. Use sparingly for roast meats, herb butters, oils, vinegars.
○, E, 1 × 1m/3 × 3ft

SORREL
(*Rumex acetosa*)
Acidic plant to be grown in quantity for use in sorrel soup and sauce. Broad leaves useful for wrapping foods. 60 × 60cm/2 × 2ft

BUCKLER LEAF SORREL
(*Rumex scutatus*)
Smaller arrowhead leaves have a sharp citrus tang. Good for green salads, vegetable soups, omelettes, sauces for fish.
30 × 60cm/1 × 2ft

THYME
(*Thymus vulgaris*)
Many edible and decorative varieties. The culinary forms are used for stock, marinades, oils, sauces and soups.
○, E, 30 × 30cm/1 × 1ft

SALAD BURNET
(*Sanguisorba minor*)
Cucumber-flavoured leaves which can be used in salads and sauces. Iced fruit drinks benefit from the cooling taste of this herb.
30 × 30cm/1 × 1ft

GREEN SAGE
(*Salvia officinalis*)
Good bee plant. Use in moderation for stuffings, sausages, pork dishes, to flavour cheese. Batter leaves and fry.
○, E, 60 × 60cm/2 × 2ft

WINTER SAVORY
(*Satureja montana*)
A few chopped leaves with broad (fava) beans or a bean casserole add a tangy spicy flavour.
38 × 30cm/15in × 1ft

ANNUAL *and* BIENNIAL HERBS

DILL
(*Anethum graveolens*)
A tall elegant feathery leaved annual with umbels of tiny aromatic blooms. Aniseed flavoured leaves are used in salads and fish dishes, and the flowers and seeds for pickles, especially cucumbers and gherkins.
60 × 15cm/2ft × 6in

CHERVIL
(*Anthriscus cerefolium*)
Use in soups, sauces, salads, egg dishes and to decorate food. An annual, left to its own cycle it will self-sow.
25 × 25cm/10 × 10in

CELERY LEAF
(*Apium graveolens*)
Use this celery-flavoured annual in soups, casseroles, pickles, curries, salads and sandwiches. Rich in vitamins and minerals.
60cm/2ft

BORAGE
(*Borago officinalis*)
Superb bee plant. Self-seeds. Bright blue star flowers to decorate food and drinks. Annual.
75 × 30cm/2½ × 1ft

CARAWAY
(*Carum carvi*)
Ancient findings of caraway show it has been used for centuries. Seeds sprinkled over meats, goose, beef stew, soups, breads, cakes. Biennial. 60 × 30cm/2 × 1ft

WILD CHICORY
(*Cichorium intybus*)
Bi/perennial with beautiful powder blue flowers which attract bees and butterflies. Root dug, cleaned, roasted and then ground makes chicory coffee.
1 × 1m/3 × 3ft

CORIANDER
(*Coriandrum sativum*)
This pungent herb has been used medicinally, as an aphrodisiac and by the Chinese for immortality! We use it now more for its culinary virtues. Annual.
60 × 30cm/2 × 1ft

SWEET BASIL
(*Ocimum basilicum*)
Grow in a heated
glasshouse and only plant
out when weather is warm.
Protect from heavy rain,
bruises easily. Tender
annual. 45 × 30cm/1½ × 1ft

PURPLE BASIL
(*Ocimum basilicum* var.
purpurascens)
Use purple basil in sauces,
salads especially tomato
salads with mozzarella
cheese. 30 × 30cm/1 × 1ft

GREEK BUSH BASIL
(*Ocimum basilicum* var.
minimum 'Greek')
A good variety to grow in
pots on the window-sill,
with miniature highly
aromatic leaves.
20 × 20cm/10 × 10in

CURLED PARSLEY
(*Petroselinum crispum*)
Garnish herb. Raw in salads
and sandwiches, cooked in
egg dishes, soups and fish.
Breath freshener. Biennial.
30 × 15cm/1ft × 6in

FLAT LEAF PARSLEY
(*Petroselinum hortense*)
Has the same properties as
the curled but a larger plant
with a stronger flavour.
60 × 30cm/2 × 1ft

SUMMER SAVORY
(*Satureja hortensis*)
Stronger flavour than
winter savory. Delicate
pink/purple flowers attract
bees. Upright growth like a
small tree. Use as winter
variety, for bean and tomato
dishes especially. Pot-pourri.
30 × 30cm/1 × 1ft

ANNUAL *and* BIENNIAL HERBS

Dill tea is extensively used
in Scandinavian countries as
an aid to digestion.

Curled parsley is a valuable
source of vitamins and
minerals, and is good for
the skin.

A pot of basil on the
window-sill will deter flies.

THE VEGETABLE GARDEN *in* SPRING

SPRING IS A BUSY TIME in the vegetable garden. When the soil is sufficiently dry to be worked, it should be dug over and raked to a fine tilth ready for seed-sowing or planting out of seedlings. If you apply fertiliser, this should be done at least three weeks before sowing.

The first pea seedlings appear in late spring. As they develop they will be given twigs for support.

◆ *Birds often devour spring crops. Protection is advisable, as shown here.*

SPRING SCHEDULE

1. Sow under glass or in heat for early crops. Plant outside when worst of frosts are past.	Summer cabbage, cauliflower, celery, leeks, lettuce.
2. Sow under glass in heat and plant out only when all frosts are past.	Runner beans, courgettes (zucchini), maize, outdoor tomatoes.
3. Sow direct into the soil when it has become manageable and worst of frosts are past.	Broad (fava) beans, beetroot, broccoli, Brussels sprouts, cabbage (summer and winter), carrots, cauliflower, celery, kale, leeks, lettuce, onion sets, parsnips, peas, radishes, salad onions, spinach, turnips.
4. Sow direct into the soil when worst of frosts are past, but protect from frost by earthing up.	Potatoes.
5. Sow direct into the soil.	French beans, runner beans, courgettes (zucchini), maize.

CROP ROTATION

If you grow the same crops in the same position year after year, you encourage a build-up of the pests that prey on the crops and deplete the soil of nutrients. A regular annual rotation will help overcome the problem. Here we show a simple three-year system. None of the crops within each group should be planted in the same position as any of the others in the group for at least three years.

Group 1 Peas, beans, onions, leeks, celery.

Group 2 Brassicas (cabbages, cauliflowers etc.), turnips.

Group 3 Mixed crops – carrots, parsnips, beetroot, courgettes (zucchini), potatoes.

Grow quick-growing crops like lettuces and radishes with any of the groups as space becomes available.

VEGETABLES

A WELL MANAGED VEGETABLE PLOT is a joy to the eye and the stomach. Home-grown vegetables are fresher, and often tastier than those in the shops, and of course the level of chemical use is entirely the gardener's choice. Beware, though, beginner's enthusiasm; the larger the plot, the more maintenance it will require. Most vegetables are grown as annuals, but if the same type of crop were grown in the same spot for several years it would drain the soil of nutrients as well as attract pests and diseases. Crops should therefore be rotated.

Heavy soils should be dug in the autumn, incorporating plenty of well rotted compost or manure. For lighter soils it may be preferable to spread the organic matter on top as a mulch, and allow the frost to do its work, digging in the spring. The soil should then be raked to a fine tilth before planting.

While raising from seed is the most economical method of growing vegetables, for those without a greenhouse or much spare time it is possible to buy seedlings ready for planting out. All the brassicas, tomatoes, lettuces, beans and courgettes can be cultivated in this way.

PEAS
Sow early to mid-spring, at intervals, in a flat-bottomed trench 15cm/6in wide and 5cm/2in deep, in 3 rows 5cm/2in apart. Support seedlings with twigs, adding netting or rows of string on upright stakes as plants grow taller.
Harvest early to midsummer, about 3 weeks after flowering.

BROAD (FAVA) BEANS
Sow late winter under glass, spring outdoors, 20cm/8in apart in double rows, with 60–90cm/2–3ft between. Sow 5–7.5cm/2–3in deep, with a dibber. Support with string tied to stakes at the corners of the row. Pinch out the top of the plant when in full flower, to discourage blackfly.
Harvest regularly from early summer, when beans are 20cm/8in long.

RUNNER BEANS
Sow from late spring onwards, 5cm/2in deep and 15cm/6in apart, in double rows 30cm/12in apart. Support plants with canes, one per plant, pushed into the soil at an angle and tied to its opposite cane a short way from the top. Pinch out the main tip when plants are 30cm/12in tall.
Harvest summer to early autumn, when beans are 15–20cm/6–8in long.

FRENCH BEANS
Sow indoors in early spring, outdoors in spring. Sow 5cm/2in deep, 7.5cm/3in apart in single rows 45cm/1½ft apart. Thin to 15cm/6in apart. Keep well watered at all times. Stake climbing varieties and pinch out the main tips when they reach the top of the canes.
Harvest midsummer onwards when beans are 10cm/4in long.

ONIONS

Most easily grown from sets, onions are planted in mid-spring 10cm/4in apart in rows 40cm/16in apart, so that the tip just shows above the soil.
Harvest in late summer when the leaves are brittle, dry in the sun and store in a cool airy place in wire bottom trays.

SALAD ONIONS

These should be grown close together, in rich, fertile soil raked to a fine tilth.
Sow at intervals from late winter onwards, under glass until the danger of frost has passed. Sow thickly 1cm/½in deep, at 1cm/½in intervals, in rows 15cm/6in apart. Do not thin, but keep weed-free, taking care not to damage the leaves or bulbs.
Harvest as soon as the onions are big enough, and use fresh.

LEEKS

Leeks prefer soil of an open free-draining texture.
Sow seed from late winter onwards, under glass at first, thinly in shallow (5mm/¼in) drills 30cm/12in apart. Keep seedlings well weeded and thin to 15mm/¾in apart, then later to 15cm/6in apart. To get white stems, blanch them by gradually earthing up soil around the plants from early autumn.
Harvest from late autumn, as required, Leeks will tolerate frost and be edible until spring.

LETTUCE

Lettuce is available in many varieties, the cabbage or butterhead lettuce, the cos, the crisphead, and the loose leaf, cut-and-come-again varieties such as Salad Bowl and Lollo Rossa.
Sow every two weeks from mid-spring to late summer in drills 2cm/¾in deep and 30cm/12in apart. Thin to between 15cm/6in and 30cm/12in according to the size of the variety. Loose leaf lettuce is sown in a block and thinned to 5cm/2in between plants.
Harvest as soon as mature as lettuces easily 'bolt' – run to seed. With loose leaf lettuces, cut the leaves as required.
Lettuce is an ideal catch crop, that is, one which matures quickly and can be planted between rows of slower growing vegetables. Also good are radishes, salad onions and summer turnips.

CELERY (SELF-BLANCHING)

Sow indoors in early spring. Do not cover the seeds, place in a plastic bag and keep moist at 13°C/55°F. Prick out 5cm/2in apart and keep warm. Harden off the plants and plant out in early summer, in a block, 15cm/6in apart. Fix black polythene round the edge of the block to aid blanching.
Harvest celery from midsummer as required, before frost.

SPINACH

Sow in late winter under glass, spring outdoors, thinly in drills 2.5cm/1in deep and 30cm/12in apart. Thin to 15cm/6in apart. Keep well watered, especially in dry weather.
Harvest. Pick leaves off the plants as required, frequently to avoid bolting.

MAIZE (SWEET CORN)

This tender plant must have a sunny sheltered site.
Sow indoors in spring, outdoors in late spring, in twos, removing the weaker seedling. Harden off indoor plants and plant out in early summer 38cm/15in apart, in a block.
Harvest late summer, when the silks on the cobs are brown and pressing the kernels produces a milky liquid.

VEGETABLES

ASPARAGUS
Asparagus needs a well-drained rich soil in a warm, sheltered part of the garden. The previous autumn, dig in plenty of well rotted manure or compost.
Year 1 In spring dig trenches 25cm/10in deep, 30cm/12in wide, and 90cm/3ft apart. Start with one year old crowns from a reputable supplier and place them 45cm/18in apart in the trench, spreading out the roots. Cover with 7.5cm/3in of soil. Hoe the soil between the trenches regularly, each time drawing a little soil over the plants until the trench is filled. In autumn cut down the foliage and apply a mulch.
Year 2 Apply a general fertilizer in spring and cut and mulch again in autumn.
Year 3 You may now harvest, but only one or two spears from each plant, leaving the foliage to build up the plant's strength. The following years you may cut for a six week period from mid-spring.

CABBAGE
Sow summer-autumn cabbages and savoys outdoors mid to late spring 20–30cm/8–12in apart. Water generously. Spring cabbages are sown in late summer, transplanted in autumn, and fertilized from late winter.
Harvest spring and summer-autumn cabbages when ready, and savoys from early autumn.

BROCCOLI
Rich, fertile well manured soil is essential.
Sow in spring both calabrese and purple sprouting in drills 1.25cm/½in deep and 38cm/15in apart. Thin seedlings to 15cm/6in apart. Keep plants well watered.
Harvest calabrese in summer, cutting the main head while the buds are still tight and leaving the stem to produce side-shoots. Purple sprouting will be ready from the following mid-winter.

BRUSSELS SPROUTS
These will overwinter but must have a fertile soil.
Sow in a sheltered spot in early spring in drills 30cm/12in apart. Transplant when 15cm/6in high. Work in fertilizer and keep properly watered. Weed well and stake tall varieties.
Harvest from late autumn onwards, from the bottom upwards.

KALE
Grow in a sheltered part of the garden.
Sow seeds in late spring, 2.5cm/1in apart, in drills 1cm/½in deep and 20cm/8in apart. Thin to 7.5cm/3in, then to 38cm/15in when plants are 15cm/6in high. Keep well watered.
Harvest in winter, cutting small young leaves from the plant's centre as required.

CAULIFLOWER
Soil should be open and fertile.
Sow indoors in mid-winter, at 13°C/55°F. Plant out in early or mid-spring. Keep weeds down and earth up stems to keep plants firm.
Harvest from early summer, as soon as they are ready.

TURNIPS
Summer turnips must be grown rapidly and make good catch crops.
Sow outdoors in early spring, thinly in drills 1cm/½in deep and 23cm/9in apart. Thin to 7.5cm/3in, then to 15cm/6in.
Harvest summer turnips when they reach the size of a golf ball. Winter varieties will be ready in mid-autumn.

CARROTS

Sow under cloches in early winter, and at intervals from late spring to summer, in drills 15cm/6in apart. Thin to 5cm/2in, then to 10cm/4in if larger carrots are required – best done in the evening to avoid carrot fly.

Harvest from early summer, according to variety, as required.

POTATOES

Sow earlies in early spring, maincrop later, 38cm/15in apart in trenches 15cm/6in deep and 60cm/2ft apart, eyes upwards. When plants are 15cm/6in tall, draw up the soil between the rows to make ridges round them. Repeat every 3 weeks.

Harvest earlies from late summer, as required. For maincrop, remove the foliage when yellow, and lift 3 weeks later (autumn).

PARSNIPS

Sow outdoors in late winter/early spring, in drills 1cm/½in deep and 30cm/12in apart, with 3 seeds together at 15cm/6in intervals. Thin to the strongest seedling in each group.

Harvest from autumn onwards, as required, but before the ground freezes.

TOMATOES

Tomatoes are usually grown under glass in temperate climates, but may be grown outside in a sunny, sheltered spot.

Sow seed indoors in early spring and keep at a temperature of 18°C/65°F. Prick seedlings into individual pots of loam potting compost when the first pair of leaves appear, then pot on as they grow until they are in a 25cm/10in container. Tomatoes may be put outside in early summer, after hardening off. Water the pots every day and give liquid tomato feed weekly. Pinch out any side shoots and pinch out the top when the plant has eight trusses. Support the stems with canes.

Harvest in summer. Pick the ripe tomatoes with the calyx on. Any tomatoes still green at the end of the summer may be ripened indoors.

BEETROOT (GLOBE)

Sow seed clusters from mid-spring onwards 15mm/¾in deep, 12cm/5in apart in rows 30cm/12in apart. Thin to the strongest seedling. Water frequently in dry summers and weed carefully.

Harvest as required from summer onwards, when they reach the size of tennis balls.

COURGETTES (ZUCCHINI)

Fertile, well-drained soil is essential.

Sow indoors in spring in pots, outdoors in very late spring, in twos, 2.5cm/1in deep and 10cm/4in apart. Remove the weaker seedling. Feed and water liberally.

Harvest as soon as they are large enough (10cm/4in), to encourage further fruits.

RADISHES

An excellent catch crop or for children to grow.

Sow outdoors, every two weeks, from spring onwards, thinly in drills 5mm/¼in deep and 15cm/6in apart. Thin to 5cm/2in apart. Do not allow the soil to dry out.

Harvest as soon as they are ready (3–4 weeks in summer).

SOFT FRUIT

THERE ARE FEW PLEASURES of the table to equal sampling one's own home-grown raspberries or redcurrants. Almost every variety of soft fruit is more delicious when picked fresh from the garden rather than bought in the shop. A quickly perishable product, soft fruit tastes fresher, is less subject to spoilage and comes in a range of cultivars that are not so easily obtainable from commercial outlets.

Strawberries can be grown in decorative terracotta pots. Planted in each of the pouches, the fruits can trail from the container without being muddied by earth.

◆ *Place the pot in an open sunny position so that the fruit ripens around the pot, and keep the soil well-watered.*

Mulching round the stems of bush fruits will help to retain moisture and keep weeds down.

Gooseberries are hardy, easy and can be grown as standards or as cordons on a wall. They prefer a slightly acid soil. As they are so thorny, plant bushes 1.5m/5ft apart to allow yourself ample room to pick the fruit.

Blueberries require a moist acid soil. Especially ornamental in spring blossom, the blue-black berries are ready for cropping summer/autumn. Like other soft fruit, they can be grown in containers, but in the open ground can reach 1.5 × 1m/5 × 3ft. Provide a sunny sheltered spot.

A summer feast of blackberries, raspberries, redcurrants, strawberries and gooseberries. The growing of blackberries has been revolutionized by the introduction of spineless varieties to ease picking. 'Oregon Thornless' is a popular example with handsome foliage. Raspberries too have been improved with sweet-tasting autumn fruiting varieties that are good when frozen. There are also long-established yellow varieties of raspberries as well as the newer 'Fallgold'.

The tayberry and loganberry (both the result of raspberry/blackberry crosses) have rich individual flavours. Plant them 2.4m/8ft apart. Plant thornless blackberries 2.4m/8ft apart and spiny blackberries 10ft/3m apart. In all cases support the canes.

TREE FRUIT

THE INTRODUCTION of dwarfing and semi-dwarfing rootstocks has enabled gardeners to grow a wide range of fruit trees even in small gardens. Where space is very limited, it is possible also to grow fruit against walls, fences or on wires in the form of cordons, espaliers or fans. These need careful pruning. An alternative is to consider columnar varieties which take up very little space and require little or no pruning. Really compact varieties of fruit can also be grown in containers. It is essential to remember that if you grow only one fruit tree, it must be a self-fertile variety, so always check with the nurseryman whether the variety you want needs another tree to pollinate it.

Apple grown over an arch is a decorative solution to the problem of limited space.

Espaliered apple in blossom. The horizontal wires are about 2.5cm/1in from the wall to allow air to circulate.

Peaches (and nectarines, the smooth-skinned form) are usually grown as fans. Varieties of each are self-fertile. Protect against spring frosts and pollinate by hand. For full sun.

Apricot Not a proposition for most gardens in cool temperate climates, but if given a warm sheltered wall, they can be fan-trained. Cultivars are self-fertile. Where they bloom at a cold time of the year, protect them and pollinate by hand.

TREE FRUIT

Pear grown as an espalier. Make sure that your varieties pollinate each other. Even 'Conference' which is often considered self-fertile will crop better with a partner.

Plums need a sunny wall. Ensure you have suitable varieties for cross-pollination, though some varieties such as 'Victoria', are self-fertile.

Damsons are less widely grown than plums despite the merit of their hardiness. Most varieties are self-fertile. 'Pixy' which is a recent variety takes up very little room. The heavy crops make wonderful jam.

Grapevines can be grown as cordons or espaliers and will need strict training or they will take up much space.

◆ *Check with the nurseryman that your choice will grow in your district.*

Fig The tree is usually fan-trained to allow the fruit to ripen. Self-fertile and grown on its own rootstock which should be restricted to a bed of 75cm/2½ft when planted. Not fully hardy and only for areas with a long warm growing season.

Morello cherry is a self-fertile acid variety for fan training on a shady wall. Ethereally lovely in spring.

3. DECORATIVE
VEGETABLES AND
SALAD HERBS

*Vegetables and herbs need not always
look dull. There are many that will
decorate both garden and table.*

Decorative Plants

The leaves of courgette (zucchini) are as decorative as the flowers. This plant has been given a place of honour in a raised bed formed of ornamental tiles.

Courgettes (zucchini) are combined in a suitable partnership with nasturtium. The female flowers develop into vegetables which should be cropped when still small, and regularly, to ensure a continuous supply. If you find that courgettes are not developing on female flowers, pollinate by dusting the pollen of the male flower onto the stigma at the centre of the female flower.

MANY VEGETABLES AND SALAD CROPS are handsome enough to be almost designer items in the kitchen garden, or, equally, in herbaceous borders. Attractive leaves, stems, pods, or flowers qualify them for both. A careful choice of these varieties will ensure that the kitchen garden is full of colour. There are for example purple-podded peas, red and white runner (stick) beans, and red forms of cabbage, lettuce and Brussels sprouts. Add to these the dark opal basil (*Ocimum basilicum* 'Dark Opal') and the magnificent silver-leaved cardoons or globe artichokes, and the scene will rival the flower garden.

DECORATIVE PLANTS

Ruby chard has red stems and veins in its leaves. Sow in spring in 2cm/1in drills which are 37.5cm/15in apart. Place the seed at 10cm/4in intervals and thin to 30cm/1ft. Or give the seed similar treatment but sow in drifts so that the crop makes patches of colour rather than straight lines. Pull when the stems are still small so that they are tender to eat.

Seakale This is the form named *Crambe maritima* and is worth growing in the flower garden. The stalks can be blanched and forced under pots like rhubarb.

◆ *It is more often grown for its glorious inflorescence which is not edible.*

DECORATIVE PLANTS

EVEN ORDINARY VEGETABLES can be turned into decoration if they are seen as architectural features and as elements in a pattern. An extra dimension can also be added if you include ornamental relatives of our usual everyday vegetables. Not all of these are worth eating and some are, be warned, inedible but their looks merit a place.

An array of ornamental brassica in pink, red, purple or white. These make stunning container plants. They are not eaten.

◆ *They can be treated as hardy annuals.*

Wigwams of runner (stick) beans and sweet peas provide height, colour and scent.

Courgettes (zucchini) are treated as potted foliage plants and placed either side of a fuchsia.

◆ *Pots are ideal for maintaining a succession in a narrow bed like this.*

Carrot leaves make a feathery edging around a heart of marigolds (tagetes), useful for deterring carrot fly.

An integrated garden where phlox flowers overhang the green erect leaves of parsnips.

Tansy (*Tanacetum vulgare*) is a decorative flowering herb and can be introduced into herbaceous beds. It tends to be invasive.

Even humble leeks can look architecturally handsome when they are grown as a mono-planting.

Climbing gourds are not edible but can be grown for decoration.

◆ *The ornate gourds can be harvested for use in the house.*

The little blue flowers of borage, orange pot marigold, heartsease and nasturtiums can be combined with other ordinary salad ingredients of the kitchen garden.

THERE IS AN ANCIENT TRADITION of eating certain flowers or using them for colour, flavour and decoration in food. This justifies including them in the kitchen garden and, since many of them are highly ornamental in themselves, they can only embellish its appearance. A good selection enables you to use them for different purposes, from flavouring vinegar to making jam or ice-cream or decorating cakes.

EDIBLE FLOWERS

GROWING FROM SEED

The international seedsman, Thompson & Morgan, sells a seed packet of edible flowers. The contents vary from season to season and are usually given on the back of the packet. As an example, previous seed packets have contained borage, *Bellis* 'White Carpet' (a large-flowered form of the daisy), pot marigold (*Calendula officinalis*), in orange, cream or yellow, heartsease (*Viola tricolor*), a form of bergamot (*Monarda citriodora*) and nasturtium.

A beautiful flower petal salad makes the centrepiece of any summer meal. This one contains the flowers of chives, marjoram, nasturtium, borage, pot marigold petals on a bed of gingermint leaves, red orach, buckler leaf sorrel, salad rocket and salad burnet leaves.

Chives (*Allium schoenoprasum*) The small mauve flowerheads which bloom in early summer are added to salads.

Pot marigold (*Calendula officinalis*) The petals can be used instead of expensive saffron. Add them fresh to salads.

Borage (*Borago officinalis*) is a beautiful sprawling annual, shown here to effect beside a pink standard rose.

◆ *The flowers are floated in cold drinks or added to salads. They can be crystallized and used as ornaments for a cake.*

Lavender The flowerheads can be added to vinegar or oil which they will flavour. Otherwise, they can be crystallized.

Fennel (*Foeniculum vulgare*) When the flowers ripen into seeds, they are sometimes used to flavour fish dishes that are baked in the oven.

Courgette (**Zucchini**) A fashionable way of eating the large melon-orange flowers is to dip them in batter and fry them.

EDIBLE FLOWERS

Roses The petals can be used in several ways as food, but take care to remove the bottom of the petal (where it joins the stalk) first. The petals can be crystallized to make a cake decoration, or cooked for rose petal jam.

ROSE PETAL JAM

Add orange-juice and lemon juice (2 table-spoonfuls of each) to 150ml (¼ pint) of water and boil together with 500gm (1 lb) of white sugar to make a syrup. Chop finely the red rose petals which you have already gently washed and dried, and add to the mixture and simmer for about half an hour, stirring continuously. Pot into little sterilized jars and seal.

Heartsease (*Viola tricolor*) Once introduced, this is a permanent, charming member of the garden as it self-seeds. Use the flowers in salads.

◆ *When you use flowers as food, whether fresh or cooked, be sure that they have not been sprayed with chemicals.*

4. Gathering and Drying

Pick flowers from the herb garden when they are at their best and dry them for months of pleasure.

DRIED FLOWERS

Flowers are hung up by their stems, head down, in an even temperature to dry. These are feverfew, fennel flowerheads in a muslin bag to catch the seeds, and oregano.

IT IS IMPORTANT TO CHOOSE the right moment to pick flowers for drying. To begin with, they must be in peak condition. There must be no trace of bruising which creates fungal problems, nor of mildew which will spread contamination. Choose a dry spell and gather them after the dew has left them, for dew-moisture will cause troubles from mould; yet you must also pick them before the mid-day sun which will rob them of their volatile oils.

Use scissors or secateurs so that you cut their stems cleanly and then place them in a large basket or box. Put them on a table and sort them into bunches, making sure you pull off any dead or pest-damaged leaves, but leave foliage which is in good condition on the plant. Keep your bunches of flowers thin because they will dry more quickly. Also, any suspicion of mould in the middle is less likely to spread early or undetected.

Hang them up to dry, head down, in an airy place at a steady temperature. An airing cupboard may be suitable, but the place doesn't have to be dark, so long as it is out of direct sunlight which will drain the colour and oils.

A basket of fresh feverfew, oregano, yarrow and mint ready for drying.

Lady's mantle (*Alchemilla mollis*), monarda, rosemary, dill flowerheads and buddleja mint.

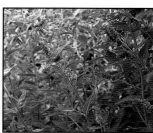

Buddleja mint is an aromatic plant with flowers which look remarkably like the butterfly bush (*Buddleja davidii*).

An enchanting barrow of dried flowers. Seed heads, teasels and flowering grasses are used both as fillers in arrangements and to give structure and shape.

◆ *The colours of dried flowers are so subtle that in combination they look like a tapestry.*

DRIED FLOWERS

Artichoke heads have interesting textures and are good for grand displays. They can be coloured or gilded.

Lavender This is the 'Hidcote' form of lavender which has quite short stems, and is a rich purple with a strong scent.

Love-in-a-mist (*Nigella*) is a good shape for decorations and its colour will mix with others. It is an annual and easy to grow from seed.

A display of leek heads, roses, safflowers, oregano, alchemilla, columbine, teasels, yarrow and feverfew.

Bistort (*Persicaria*) produces two crops of shaggy pink flowerheads a year. Pick it in quantity for a massed display.

Chives (*Allium schoenoprasum*) lose their onion scent when dried. They produce two crops of flowerheads a year.

Monarda can be grown in pink, scarlet or purple forms. The bergamot scent remains even when the flowers are dried.

A colourful mass of chives, flax, alchemilla, sea-holly (eryngium), lavender, miniature roses, oregano, golden rod and leek heads.

5. CREATIVE IDEAS

The flowers and leaves of the herb garden can decorate the house and fill it with fragrance.

SPRING *and* SUMMER

THE FLOWERS OF MANY HERBS are so decorative and colourful that they are worth cutting to make wonderful fresh flower arrangements.

A mug of herbs composed of lavender, pot marjoram, rosemary, monarda, red sage, applemint and opal basil.

Southernwood (*Artemisia abrotanum*) forms the basis of this arrangement, layered according to size, gathered at the base, tied with hessian ribbon and wired at the back to hang.

The flowers of chives, lavender, marigold (calendula) and meadowsweet (filipendula) in a simple but dramatic arrangement.

A posy of anise hyssop, rosemary, honeysuckle, lavender, lady's mantle, pot marjoram, red sage and meadowsweet.

A sunburst of lavender flowerheads.

A decorated watering-can of dill heads, fennel heads, southernwood, rosemary, mint, yarrow, golden tansy, feverfew and oregano.

POT-POURRI

THE ORIGINAL PURPOSE of pot-pourri was to mask odours and for this reason it was strewn about the house. Nowadays it is used to scent rooms or to put into sachets or bags as pretty gifts, or to put into cushions or pillows (with a double lining to protect the contents).

A SPICY POT-POURRI

1. The ingredients are the dried petals of sunflowers, pot marigolds, safflowers and lavender, bay leaves, chillies, cinnamon sticks, orange peel, ginger root, cloves and star anise.

2. Mix all the flower petals together to form a base, then add the lavender.

3. Break up the bay leaves into the bowl, releasing their aroma, add the chillies, break up the orange peel, cinnamon sticks, ginger root, star anise and finally add the cloves.

4. Stir the ingredients together to mix the aromas. It should last in the open bowl and provide fragrance for at least six months.

When you have made your pot-pourri, the ideal container is one with a lid such as a ginger jar or crock pomander. Open bowls or baskets are often used but the pot-pourri will have a shorter lifespan as the light and constant exposure to the air will break down the fragrance and destroy the colours. With a ginger jar you can take off the lid and stir the pot-pourri to expel the natural perfumes into the room when needed, replacing the lid after use.

A Pot-Pourri Ball

For this you need a shallow box, latex glue and a styrofoam ball (consisting of dried oasis which is available from florists). Fill the bottom of the box with pot-pourri. Push a knitting needle through the centre of the styrofoam ball, then coat the ball in latex glue and roll it through the pot-pourri. Allow it to dry. Repeat the process three times until the ball is completely covered. When it is finished, hang it on a ribbon.

Flowers for a Colourful Pot-Pourri

Alkanet, borage, cornflowers, delphiniums, feverfew, pot marigolds, mullein, pansy, primroses, polyanthus, tansy.

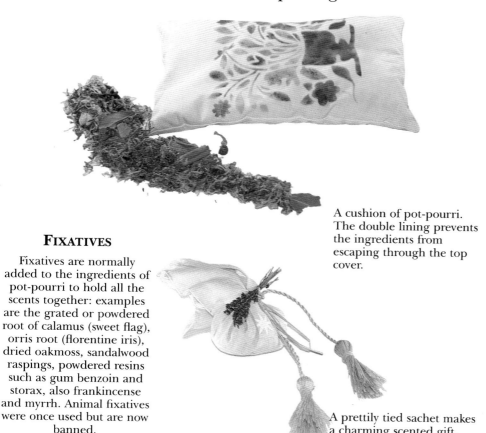

A cushion of pot-pourri. The double lining prevents the ingredients from escaping through the top cover.

Fixatives

Fixatives are normally added to the ingredients of pot-pourri to hold all the scents together: examples are the grated or powdered root of calamus (sweet flag), orris root (florentine iris), dried oakmoss, sandalwood raspings, powdered resins such as gum benzoin and storax, also frankincense and myrrh. Animal fixatives were once used but are now banned.

A prettily tied sachet makes a charming scented gift.

SUMMER *and* AUTUMN

BY AUTUMN, the garden will have yielded most of its flowers and fruits. This is the richest time for gathering materials such as seed pods, flowers, warmly coloured leaves, cones, nuts, rose hips, hops and fruits. These will make delightful decorations for the kitchen or creative small gifts.

An imposing arrangement with oak leaves and the heads of globe artichoke. It makes good use of seed heads, including poppies and nigella and the graceful foxtail grass (*Setaria glauca*).

A pot-pourri tree which is made in the same way as the pot-pourri ball, on a styrofoam cone. It is set in plaster of Paris with a hazel twig forming the trunk.

A tree made from Icelandic moss. Use little hooks of florist's wire to fix it to a styrofoam cone. The 'flowers' are dried *Achillea* 'Cloth of Gold'.

A plaited rope of garlic is always useful and decorative in any kitchen.

Ornamental gourds, although they are not edible, are well worth growing for autumn and winter decoration. Dry them thoroughly and paint them with a matt varnish to prolong their life.

A swag of flowers, dried fruits, breads (made with a salt dough and then dried), snail shells, cones, *bouquet garni*, chillies, root ginger and cinnamon sticks.

◆ *The base could be plaited cane, straw or a wood which is light enough to hang. If you use a glue gun, you can fix a wide variety of materials.*

75

WINTER

A glue gun, which heats the glue before it touches the surface, is the best tool for this kind of work.

WINTER DECORATIONS should brighten the dullness of the season with warming hues and heady scents. Consider spices, pine cones and dried citrus as well as shrubby evergreen herbs and fruits from the garden. For a flamboyant effect, some flowers and seed heads can be silvered or gilded to reflect the light.

A large cone can be used successfully to make a miniature tree decorated with seed pods, spices, shells, herbs and flowers.

Winter tree decorations made of miniature reeds and flower pots with herbs and spices – a lively and original treatment.

◆ *If stored in airtight tins, these will last for several years.*

Flowers dried the previous summer will certainly provide a display although you cannot expect them to last more than about a year.

A traditional clove pomander, made by sticking whole cloves into a firm fresh orange so that they are densely packed. Dry the pomander in a warm moistureless atmosphere and this fragrant ball will last for a number of years.

An interesting sphere made from cane. A selection of spices and herbs have been stuck to it.

Some dried flowers, particularly those with large heads and seeds, can be enhanced if you spray them with gold or bronze paint.